ON THE SHORE
OF WEST LAKE

西子湖畔

FOREIGN LANGUAGES PRESS   BEIJING

外文出版社 北京

ON THE SHORE OF WEST LAKE

When you fly over Hangzhou during the day and look down, you will be surprised to see a lake shimmering like a bright pearl below. This is the famous West Lake.

Comparing West Lake to a pearl is a good simile; it also coincides with an age-old legend, which says that in remote antiquity when Jade Dragon and Golden Phoenix were polishing a piece of precious jade by the Heavenly River, the jade was transformed into a bright pearl that sparkled in heaven. Upon hearing about it, the Queen Mother of the West sent someone to take away the pearl for herself. Jade Dragon and Golden Phoenix went to see her and demanded it back. During the subsequent scramble for it, the pearl fell down, landed on the western side of the city of Hangzhou and became West Lake. Jade Dragon and Golden Phoenix also came down to the lakeside and became Jade Emperor's Hill and Phoenix Hill that guard the lake day and night.

A fable as it is, the story, however, told a truth. It was long years of polishing that transformed West Lake into a bright pearl. Jade Dragon and Golden Phoenix who polished it were none other than the people of Hangzhou. In the long-distant past, West Lake was a bay at the mouth of the Qiantang River. The bay was later silted up and became a lagoon. The first signs of a lake appeared 1800 years ago. In the year 591, after the seat of the Hangzhou county government was moved to the foot of Phoenix Hill, people began to remould West Lake. During the Tang dynasty (618-907), when the great poet Bai Juyi served as the governor of Hangzhou, he dredged the lake and built causeways. He also went on pleasure trips there and wrote poems about the lake. As a result, the lake became famous throughout the country. Later, under the guidance of Su Dongpo, Yang Mengying and Ruan Yuan, isles, causeways, pavilions, terraces and other structures, which embodied traditional Chinese cultural ideals and were wholly compatible with the basic quality of the local landscape, were built, transforming West Lake, a lake created by nature, into a lake better than nature's creation, a lake with a rich cultural content and more elegant and attractive. With cloud-enshrouded hills on three sides and a city on one side, West Lake is located at a spot that conveys the feeling of both solidity and openness, magnificence and delicacy, a place of perfect structural beauty with appropriate degrees of openness and closeness. Emphasis is laid on curved lines with green and dark green as the key colours. The beautiful isles and causeways and elegant pavilions and terraces give the scenery refreshing reliefs. Although many of the structures are man-made, they do not look so, because they melt naturally with nature and have become parts of nature. There are appropriate open spaces for the comfort of the eyes and for pacifying the mind, an arrangement that represents the beauty of the golden mean and peace of mind in philosophy. The lake is close to a city, and yet far away from the crowd, where people can find joy and inspirations in a harmonious union between man and nature, a union of heaven, earth and man. It leads one into dreams and yearnings, in which one is intoxicated by the beauty of the environment. For this reason, West Lake has become a rare classic in China's landscape culture. Its beauty is inexhaustible and varied in different seasons, time of the day, weather and spaces. There are endless scenic wonders. The great poet Su Dongpo (1037-1101) of the Song dynasty, wrote that West Lake "is always perfectly beautiful whether heavily made up or lightly rouged." "As its beauty in different shades is to be found everywhere, how can we see all of it?"

The beauty of West Lake has marvelled many a visitor from overseas both in the past and present. More than 400 years ago, a Japanese envoy said with emotion, "I saw a picture of the lake in the past and did not believe there was such a lake in the human world. When I pass by the lake today, I found the painter of the picture was lacking in skill." Marco Polo, the famous 13th- century Venetian traveller, praised Hangzhou as "the most beautiful and noble city in the world" on account of the beauty of West Lake and prosperity of the city of Hangzhou. Disaster nearly befell on Hangzhou in history because of the beauty of West Lake. During the Northern Song dynasty (960-1127), the poet Liu Yongzeng extolled the beauty of Hangzhou and West Lake in his poem *Watching Sea Tide*. Later, after reading the poem, the Kin ruler Wanyan Liang (reigning 1149-1161) sent a painter secretly into the Hangzhou to paint pictures of the scenic attractions of West Lake before he led his army in a southward march. When he saw the pictures painted by the painter, he was overwhelmed with joy. He had the pictures framed on a screen and added a picture of himself riding on a horse on top of Wushan Hill on the shore of West Lake and wrote these words: "Leading an army of a million, I ride my horse to the top the first peak of Wushan Hill."

The beautiful West Lake has attracted many public figures to Hangzhou. Most of the famous poets in Chinese history had been at West Lake and written thousands of poems about it. Hangzhou was the capital of the state of Wuyue (907-978) and the Southern Song dynasty (1127- 1279). Emperor Lizong of the Southern Song dynasty and Emperor Kangxi of the Qing dynasty had an imperial travelling palace and garden built on Solitary Hill, where "the scenery of lake and hill is at its best." In the last half of a century, Hangzhou has played host to as many as 100 heads of governments and leaders of states, including Richard Nixon, Georges Pompidou and Margaret Thatcher. On the shore of West Lake are many former residences and graves of famous Chinese poets, painters, scholars and national heroes, which lend historic interest to West Lake.

The beauty of West Lake is embodied in its many attractions. In addition to the 10 traditional attractions that date back more than 800 years, there are now 10 new attractions elected in modern times. Around the lake, there are also famous gardens and parks, such as Guozhuang, Liuzhuang, Wangzhuang, Xiling Seal Engraving Society, Zhongshan Park and Princes Bay Park; famous springs, such as Dragon Well, Tiger-Dug Spring and Jade Fountain; famous hills, such as Solitary Hill, South Peak and Five-Cloud Hill; famous caves, such as Stone House, Misty Cloud, Cloud-Hovering and Lingshan caves; famous temples, such as Lingyin, Jingci, Santianzhu and Phoenix temples; famous sites, such as Pagoda of Six Realms, Flying-in Peak, Rocky Grottoes, ruins of the imperial palace on Phoenix Hill, Crane-Keeping Pavilion and Hall of Flourishing Literature; famous museums, such as Zhejiang Museum, China Tea Museum, China Silk Museum, Zhejiang Hu Qingyu's Museum of Chinese Medicine and Museum of Government Porcelain Kilns of the Southern Song Dynasty.

西子湖畔

当您白天乘坐飞机驾凌杭州上空时，一定会惊奇地俯瞰到如明珠般闪闪发光的一泓湖水，那就是著名的西湖。

将西湖比作明珠，既妙于形容，又与古老传说相合。传说远古时候，天河边的玉龙和金凤将一块宝玉琢磨成了一颗明珠。明珠光耀天宇，惊动了天上的王母娘娘，遂派员将明珠窃为己有。玉龙、金凤向王母索还，争夺过程中，明珠不慎跌落，坠在杭州城西，形成西湖。玉龙与金凤也双双飞落到西湖畔，成为玉皇山与凤凰山，日夜守候在西湖边。

这虽是传说，但道出了一个真理：西湖确是经过长期琢磨才成为明珠的，琢磨她的"玉龙"、"金凤"就是杭州人民。远古时，西湖仅是钱塘江口的一个海湾，后经泥沙淤积而成泻湖，1800年前才出现湖的雏形。公元591年杭州县治移至凤凰山麓以后，人们开始逐步改造西湖。唐代（公元618－907年）时，大诗人白居易任杭州刺史时曾疏浚西湖、修筑湖堤，并常游乐其间，歌吟西湖，使之名噪天下。以后，西湖在苏东坡、杨孟瑛、阮元等各朝守杭的"士大夫"们的指导下，按照其山水基本品质，巧妙地营建了一些堤岛亭台等设施，注入了中国传统文化的理念，使西湖源于自然，胜于自然，更富文化意蕴，更秀雅动人。西湖"三面云山一面城"，三面聚合，一面通透，既大气又灵动，具有开合得宜的结构美；她以曲线为要素，以青绿为基调，堤岛秀丽，亭台雅致，具有秀雅清丽的气质美；她虽经人类加工，但不露斧痕，不失真趣，不失天性，具有自然自在的艺术美；她空间适度，视觉舒适，令人心平气和，具有中庸平和的哲理美；她虽紧贴城市，却远离了尘嚣，令人融入自然，获得人与自然和谐共生的愉悦和灵悟，具有天人合一的功能美；她给人梦幻，让人憧憬，使人陶醉于美好境界之中……西湖于是成为中国山水文化罕见的经典。她的美，没有穷尽，在不同的时节、不同的时间、不同的气候、不同的空间里都具有不同的美，变化无穷，佳境不绝。宋代大文豪苏东坡（公元1037－1101年）称西湖是"淡妆浓抹总相宜"。认为西湖之美："深浅随所得，岂能识其全。"

西湖的美让古今海外游客震惊。400多年前一位日本使者曾感叹："昔年曾见此湖图，不信人间有此湖。今日打从湖上过，画工还欠着工夫。"13世纪意大利著名旅行家马可·波罗因西湖之美和杭州城之繁华而赞美杭州是"世界上最美丽华贵之城"。历史上杭州也差一点因西湖的美丽而遭难：北宋（公元960－1127年）诗人柳永曾作《望海潮》词赞美杭州及西湖，后被金主完颜亮（公元1149－1161年在位）所闻，在率兵南侵之前，特地派遣画工潜入杭州，画下西湖名胜。完颜亮见图大喜，命人制成屏风，画上自己策马立于西湖边的吴山绝顶上，并题上了"提兵百万西湖上，立马吴山第一峰。"

西湖的美吸引了各方名人会聚杭州。中国历史著名诗人大多游历过西湖，留下了成千上万的诗篇。吴越国（公元907－978年）和南宋王朝（公元1127－1279年）还将国都定在杭州。南宋理宗皇帝和清帝康熙还都在西湖"湖山绝胜处"孤山建立了行宫与御花园。近半个世纪以来，杭州接待过尼克松、蓬皮杜、撒切尔夫人等各国首脑与元首上百位。在西子湖畔，留下了许多中国著名诗人、画家、学者、民族英雄的故居与墓群，也为西湖增色。

西湖之美体现在丰富的景观之中。这里有800多年前就形成的传统景观"西湖十景"，也有当代评选出来的"新西湖十景"。此外，还有郭庄、刘庄、汪庄、西泠印社、中山公园、太子湾公园等名园，龙井、虎跑、玉泉等名泉，孤山、南高峰、五云山等名山，石屋洞、烟霞洞、栖霞洞、灵山洞等名洞，灵隐、净慈、三天竺、凤凰寺等名寺，六和塔、飞来峰石窟、凤凰山皇宫遗址、放鹤亭、文澜阁等名迹，以及浙江博物馆、中国茶叶博物馆、中国丝绸博物馆、杭州胡庆余堂中药博物馆、南宋官窑博物馆等名馆。

West Lake, a lake of 5.6 square kilometres in the western part of Hangzhou in Zhejiang Province, is surrounded by hills on three sides with the city of Hangzhou on one side.

西湖，位于浙江省杭州市西部，三面环山，一面傍城，面积5.6平方公里。

Sunset on the lake.
湖滨夕照

West Lake is screened by gauze-like tender green willows in spring.
春风又绿江南岸。西湖岸柳新绿，似碧纱轻笼。

Green willows interspersed with pink peach ▷
blossoms add infinite colour to spring.

"一株杨柳一株桃"，桃红柳绿，春色无尽。

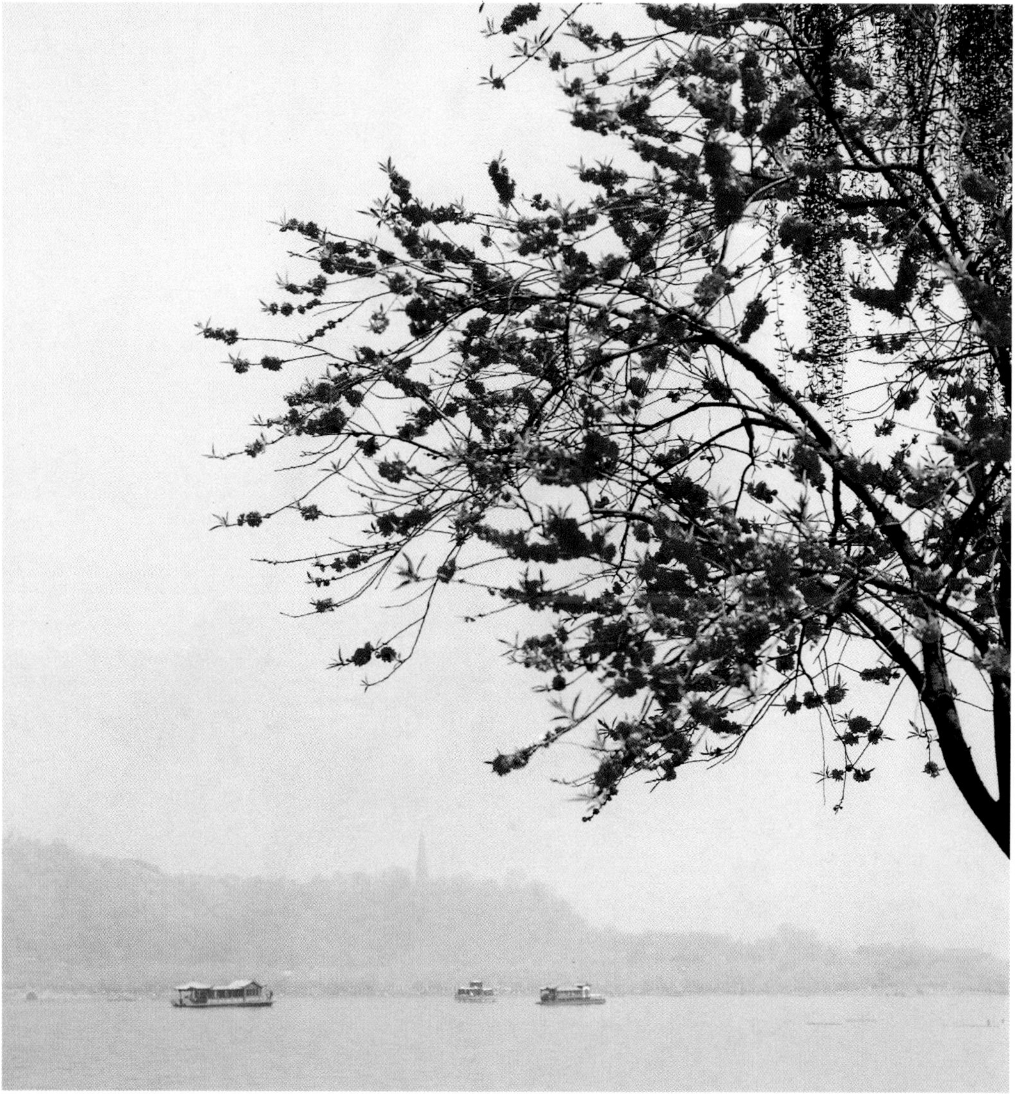

Baoshu Pagoda

In the year 975. Jian Liu, king of the state of Wuyue, was summoned to the capital by the emperor and did not return for a long time. His ministers built the pagoda to pray for his safe return. The pagoda standing gracefully like a young maiden has become a landmark of Hangzhou.

保俶塔

公元975年吴越王钱镠奉召进京，久留未返，大臣们建此塔祈祷他平安归来。其亭亭如美女，成为杭州的标志。

"A vast expanse of green are the lotus leaves that spread to the horizon; Unusually red are the flowers in the setting sun." These two lines describe summer on West Lake.

"接天莲叶无穷碧，映日荷花别样红"，是西子湖夏日胜景。

Traces of Snow on Broken Bridge

This is one of the 10 attractions of West Lake, where the world is like a jade carving.

断桥残雪

西湖十景之一，其境如琼玉世界。

Bai's Causeway

Starting from Broken Bridge, Bai's Causeway runs for a whole kilometres to Solitary Hill in the west. Walking on the causeway is like walking into a picture.

白堤

白堤东起断桥、西接孤山，全长约一公里。漫步堤上，如入画境。

Storm Pavilion and Lake Mirroring Hall

Both were built in memory of Qiu Jin, a famous woman revolutionary active during the period of democratic revolution in China. Her grave is at Xiling Bridge, a distance from here.

风雨亭与镜湖厅

都是为纪念中国民主革命时期著名女革命家秋瑾而建、秋瑾之墓，就在不远处的西泠桥畔。

Spring on Solitary Hill

An imperial travelling palace was built on the hill in the past. Standing alone in the lake and surrounded by water, Solitary Hill is known to be the place where "the scenery of lake and hill is at its best."

孤山春色

曾作为昔日帝王行宫所在地的孤山，独峙湖中，湖水萦绕，无愧于"湖山绝佳处"的殊誉。

Best View of West Lake

This was a corner of the imperial garden of several hundred years ago. A couplet describing the scenic wonders of West Lake can be read backwards or by every other word in the couplet.

西湖天下景

数百年前的御花园一角、以一副可倒读、跳读的名联道破西湖妙景而著称。

Autumn Moon on Calm Lake

This scenic spot is at the western end of Bai's Causeway. The Lake-Watching Pavilion built here in the Tang dynasty more than 1,000 years ago is still one of the best places for watching the moon at West Lake.

平湖秋月

位居白堤西端、1000多年前唐朝时就建有望湖亭、至今是西湖赏月的胜地之一。

Xiling Seal Engraving Society

This is the name of both a society and a garden. The Xiling Seal Engraving Society is a famous academic society for the study of seal making founded in the early 20th century. Because of this society, Hangzhou is known as the "seal city." The Cypress Hall in the garden was built during the period of Southern Dynasties, and the Bamboo Pavilion, built by the poet Bai Juyi.

西泠印社

既是印社名，又是园名。西泠印社创立于 20 世纪之初，是中国研究金石篆刻的著名学术团体、杭州因此而称"印城"，园中柏堂为南朝遗迹，其竹阁为白居易所筑。

Crane-Keeping Pavilion

The pavilion was built in memory of Lin Hejing (967-1029), a poet and learned scholar of the Northern Song dynasty, who refused to serve as an official, lived as a recluse on Solitary Hill and made keeping cranes and cultivating plum trees his hobbies. He never married but looked upon the plum trees as his wife and the cranes his children. The beautiful story of his life is still retold today.

放鹤亭

北宋诗人林和靖（公元 967 – 1029 年）学识卓著而终生不仕，隐居孤山，喜欢养鹤种梅，不婚娶，以梅为"妻"，以鹤为"子"，至今犹为美谈。放鹤亭为纪念他而建。

Morning over the Three Pools
The Three Pools at the centre of West Lake built by
the great poet Su Dongpo have become a landmark of
Hangzhou's West Lake.

三潭晨曦
三潭位于西湖湖心，最初为大诗人苏东坡所筑，而今
成为杭州西湖的标志。

Spring on Small Fairy Isle

Small Fairy Isle is one of the three isles in West Lake. Because of the charming scenery of isle and lake, the isle looks like the legendary dwelling of immortals.

小瀛洲之春

西湖湖中三岛之一，湖中有岛，岛中有湖，景色优美，宛如仙山琼岛。

25

Summer on Small Fairy Isle

The lotus flowers planted at Small Fairy Isle give the isle an unsullied look because the lotus flowers grow out of mud but are unsoiled by mud.

小瀛洲之夏
小瀛洲因为栽植了出淤泥而不染的荷花，更显得出俗不凡。

Autumn on Small Fairy Isle

In autumn, the gorgeous chrysanthemum flowers among exquisite structures transform Small Fairy Isle into a totally different place.

小瀛洲之秋
灿烂的秋菊，迷人的亭台，小瀛洲犹如别一世界。

Three Pools Mirroring the Moon

This is one of the 10 attractions of West Lake. On the night of the Mid-Autumn Festival, candles are lit in the stone lamp posts in the Three Pools, and the holes are covered with paper. When the candle lights are reflected in the lake, they present a wonderful picture of "a moon in the sky and three more in the lake."

三潭印月

西湖十景之一、中秋之夜，三潭塔内点烛，洞口蒙上纸，烛光外透，倒映湖中，形成"天上月一轮，湖中影成三"的奇景。

Pavilion of Complete Rapport

"My mind is in complete rapport with the truth" is a Buddhist saying, meaning that "mutual understanding is achieved without saying a word." A visitor may understand the meaning of this phrase by quietly meditating over it.

我心相印亭

"我心相印"为禅语，意即"不必言说，彼此会意"游至此地，静心体察，必有所悟。

Spring Morning on Su's Causeway

Built by Su Dongpo when he was serving as the prefect of Hangzhou more than 900 years ago, Su's Causeway is 2.8 kilometres long, planted with peach and willow trees and interspersed with six stone bridges. Spring Morning on Su's Causeway is the first one of the 10 attractions of West Lake.

苏堤春晓

苏堤，为900多年前杭州知州苏东坡所筑，全长2.8公里，堤上间植桃、柳，设六座石拱桥。"苏堤春晓"为"西湖十景"之首景。

32

Rainbow Rising Bridge
This is the first bridge at the northern end of Su's
Causeway. A colourful rainbow often rises above the
bridge when the sun comes out after rain.

跨虹桥
苏堤北侧第一桥。雨过天晴，时见彩虹缤纷。

Boat Race on West Inner Lake
West Inner Lake is a small lake on the western side of West Lake. As the water is relatively smooth here, it is an ideal place for boat race and angling.

西里湖竞舟
西里湖，为西湖西侧小湖，相对平静安宁，是竞舟、垂钓佳处。

Rainbow over Jade Ribbon

Jade Ribbon is the name of a bridge. Rainbow over Jade Ribbon is one of the 18 scenic attractions of West Lake named during the Qing dynasty. On a fine day, when the vermilion balustrade on the bridge is reflected in the water, they are like a rainbow in the lake.

玉带晴虹

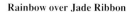

"玉带"是桥名，此景为清代西湖十八景之一。晴日、阳光映照、朱栏倒影、如长虹卧波、由此而名。

Snow-Draped Cypresses in the Curved Courtyard
Snow scene is also enchanting in this garden known for its summer scenery.

曲院杉林雪景
在以夏景闻名的公园里，雪景同样迷人。

Lotus in the Breeze in the Curved Courtyard
This is another one of the 10 attractions of West Lake. The place used to be the site of Hongchunqiao Government Brewery in the Southern Song dynasty. The brewery was moved to the shore of Yue Lake during the reign of Emperor Kangxi (1662-1722) of the Qing dynasty. The place is now a garden with lotus flowers as its special feature.

曲院风荷
西湖十景之一，南宋时为洪春桥一官酒作坊之景，清康熙年间（公元1662－1722年）迁至岳湖畔，现成荷花特色公园。

Lotus Flowers of West Lake

There are several dozen species of lotus flowers in West Lake, such as the United, A-Shaped, Zhongtai, Thousand-Petal, King and Bowl lotus flowers, which are red, white, pink or mottled-gold in colour or golden edged.

西湖荷花

西湖的荷花，有并蒂莲、品字莲、重台莲、千瓣莲、大王莲、碗莲等数十个品种，有红、白、粉红、洒金、金边等各种色彩。

Rosy Dawn on West Lake

The rosy clouds of dawn on West Lake are as gorgeous as the
brocades made in Hangzhou, a city known for its silk and satin.

西湖朝霞

西湖绚丽的朝霞，正如这个丝绸之府灿烂的云锦。

Spring Rain

The lake and hills are even more enchanting
when they are enshrouded in a misty rain.

春雨

雨中湖光山色空蒙飘渺，更觉奇美。

Fish-Watching at Flower Port

This one of the 10 attractions used to be a private garden in the Southern Song period. It is now the largest garden at West Lake noted for its gold fish and peony flowers.

花港观鱼

西湖十景之一，南宋时为私家小园，现为西湖最大的公园，以红鲤鱼与牡丹花景观著称。

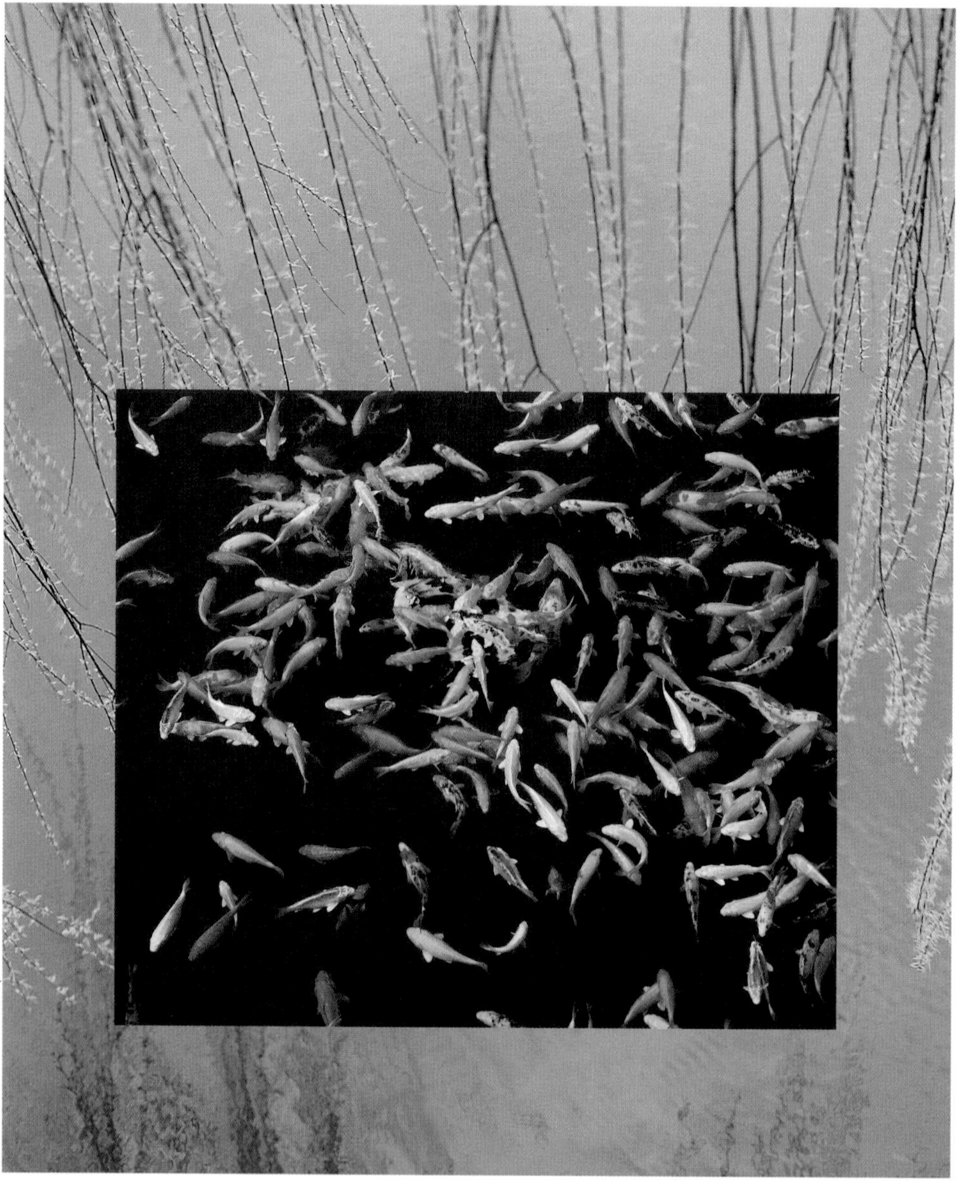

Long Corridor at Flower Port

As each section of the long corridor presents a different scene, walking down the corridor is like strolling through an art gallery.

花港长廊

这里，步移景换，成为展示花港美的画廊。

◁ **Joyous Fish**

In the fish pond at Flower Port are several hundred golden-scaled red carp. Feeding the fish in the pond is a pleasant pastime. The spot has thus become known as the Garden of Joyous Fish.

鱼乐

花港鱼池蓄养数百尾金鳞红鲤，若投饵池中，群鱼逐食、鱼乐人更乐，故称鱼乐园。

Fancy Windows

Windows of varied designs at Guozhuang frame beautiful sights.

花窗

郭庄花窗形式丰富，取景优美。

Guozhuang

This private garden of the Qing dynasty is picturesquely located by the lake with hills behind it. The garden is divided into two parts, which are named Quiet Dwelling and Mirroring the Sky, each different in scenic interest.

郭庄

为清代私家花园，背山临湖，以西湖为借景，独得其妙。园内有"静必居"宅院与"一镜天开"庭院两大部分，各有其趣。

Fragrant Snow Heralding Spring

This is the name of a hall at Guozhuang. Its elegant interior decoration and quiet atmosphere reveal the taste of the refined scholars who were engaged in easy conversation there in the past.

香雪分春

为郭庄宅院厅堂、古朴高雅、明丽幽静、仿佛还能听见当年雅士们的清谈。

49

Peony Pavilion

This pavilion is in the Peony Garden at Huagang. Below the pavilion are many rare species of peony flowers, which present a riot of colour in spring and draw all the visitors to them.

牡丹亭

为花港观鱼牡丹园中建筑，亭下有争艳斗奇的牡丹珍品，是游人春天必到之处。

Orioles Singing in Wavy Willows

This one of the 10 attractions of West Lake was at the former Jujingyuan imperial garden of the Southern Song period, known for its more than 500 willows of various species, where orioles often gather. Flower and lantern shows are held here in autumn.

柳浪闻莺

西湖十景之一、南宋时为御花园"聚景园"，荟集各种名柳 500 多株，于是黄莺汇集。该园秋季常举办各种花展与灯展。

Misty Isles in the Morning Light

When the isles in West Lake are enveloped in themorning mists, they look as unreal as the dwelling of immortals.

晨光岛影

晨光中的西湖空灵、迷蒙, 湖中之岛虚无缥缈, 犹如仙境。

◁ Cherry Blossoms on the Lake Shore

Many cherry trees are planted on the lake shore and in the gardens. Their graceful and ethereal flowers give an otherworldly touch to the beautiful scenery.

湖边樱花

西湖边或其公园里，栽植的樱花也不少，她雅丽、轻盈，给人超尘脱俗的美感。

Snow Scene on West Lake

When commenting on the scenery of West Lake, an ancient said, "The lake on a fine day is not as good as the lake in the rain; the lake in the rain, not as good as the lake under moonlight; the lake under moonlight, not as good as the lake in the snow." Snow turns West Lake into a crystal world.

西湖雪景

古人评论西湖景色说："晴湖不如雨湖，雨湖不如月湖，月湖不如雪湖。"西湖雪景，托出一个琼玉世界。

Yellow Dragon Cave

The cave was the site of a religious establishment founded by Monk Huikai in the 13th century. Becoming one of the three Taoist temples at West Lake in the late Qing period, it is now a quiet garden in the hills with many attractive views and groves of trees unconventionally and compactly laid out.

黄龙洞

为13世纪慧开禅师所创，晚清为西湖三大道院之一，现为一处幽静的山间园林，"多方胜景，咫尺山林"，别致紧凑。

Yue Fei's Temple

The temple was built to honour Yue Fei, a national hero of the Southern Song period more than 800 years ago. The temple and Yue Fei's tomb next to it are key cultural relics under state protection visited by every tourist. Yue Fei (1103-1142) was a famous general who stood for fighting and repulsing the Kin invaders. He was framed and murdered by traitors in the Song court.

岳王庙

是800多年前南宋时的民族英雄岳飞的祠堂、祠旁为岳坟、为全国重点文物保护单位。是西湖游客必到之地。岳飞(公元1103－1142年）是南宋名将，因力主抗击金兵、遭朝中权奸诬陷被杀害。

Giant Buddha in Lingyin Temple

The gilded sitting statue of Sakyamuni enshrined in the Great Buddha's Hall in Lingyin Temple is 19.6 metres high or 24.8 metres including the seat. Carved in 24 blocks of camphor wood pieced together, it is the largest gilded wooden sitting statue of the Buddha to be found in China.

灵隐大佛

灵隐寺大雄宝殿中的释迦牟尼贴金坐像，高 19.6 米，连座高 24.8 米，采用 24 块香樟木雕成，为中国最大的木雕坐式贴金佛像。

Grottoes on Flying-in Peak

The sculptural works in the grottoes on this hill represent the ancient grotto art in the southern part of China. They are key cultural relics under state protection. Altogether there are over 470 stone statues carved during the period of Five Dynasties (907-960) and Song and Yuan dynasties (1271-1368) with 335 of them in better preservation.

飞来峰石窟

为全国重点文物保护单位，中国南方古代石窟艺术的代表，雕有五代（公元 907－960 年）宋、元（公元 1271－1368 年）石刻造像 470 多尊，其中保存较好的 335 尊。

Tiger-Dug Dream Spring

The name of the spring came from Monk Xingkong of the Tang dynasty more than 1,000 years ago, who dreamed of a tiger digging into the ground and finding a spring. The sweet water from this spring is the best for making Dragon Well tea. Close to the spring are the ancient Tiger-Dug Temple, Pagoda and Temple of Monk Jigong and Memorial Hall of Li Shutong.

虎跑梦泉

1100多年前唐代性空和尚在此梦虎刨地得泉。此泉水质甘醇, 泡龙井茶特佳。泉旁有虎跑古寺、济公塔院、李叔同纪念室等。

◁**Dragon Well**

Dragon Well is one of the three famous springs of West Lake and also the name of the place where the famous Dragon Well tea is produced. Sipping Tea at Dragon Well is one of the 10 new attractions of West Lake.

龙井

为西湖三大名泉之一。龙井又为地名, 是著名龙井茶的产地。"新西湖十景"名之为"龙井问茶"。

Path Through Cloud-Enshrouded Bamboo Groves
It is said that multi-coloured auspicious clouds often drift to this spot at the foot of Five-Cloud Hill, where there are dense bamboo groves, tall ancient trees, beautiful scenery and cool shades. The area was visited by Emperor Kangxi and Emperor Qianlong (1736-1795) of the Qing dynasty.

云栖竹径
在五云山麓，传说五彩祥云常栖于此，竹林茂密，古树参天、清凉悦目、清帝康熙、乾隆（1736 – 1795 年在位）曾游于此。

Misty Trees at Nine Creeks

Nine Creeks and Eighteen Caves is a scenic area in the hills southwest of West Lake. Praising it as the best scenic area of West Lake, a Qing scholar named Yu Yuezan described it in a poem: "The serried hills roll on; the paths bend and wind; gurgling and bubbling the springs flow; high and low the trees grow."

九溪烟树

即九溪十八涧，位于西湖西南群山之间，景甚野逸。清学者俞樾赞为"西湖最胜处"并诗以述之："重重叠叠山，曲曲环环路，丁丁东东泉，高高下下树。"

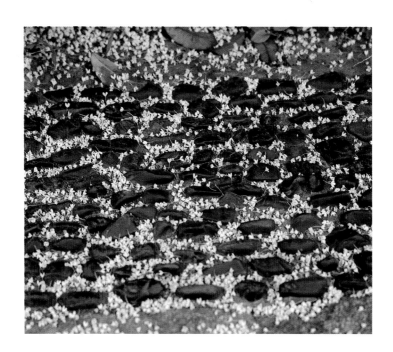

Rain of Osmanthus Flowers Filling Ditches

This is a traditional area for enjoying the sweet-scented osmanthus flowers in Hangzhou. There are as many as 10,000 osmanthus trees here, some of them more than 200 years old. Every autumn when the osmanthus flowers are the most enchanting, the spot is the main area of activities during the Hangzhou Osmanthus Festival.

满陇桂雨

杭州传统赏桂花胜地，有桂树万株，树古者逾200年，每至金秋，桂花迷人，此地为"西湖桂花节"主场址。

Snow Scenery in the Hills

There are many secluded spots in the hills around West Lake. Scenery at these places is even more inspiring when they are covered with snow.

山中雪景

环西湖山中，幽境殊多，著雪尤妙，清韵无限。

Jingci Temple

Built in 954 at the foot of Nanping Hill, this is one of the four great temples of West Lake. As the sound of the bells in the temple can be heard as far as in the city of Hangzhou. "Evening Bells of Nanping" has become of one of the 10 attractions of West Lake.

净慈寺

创建于公元954年，为"西湖四大丛林"之一。寺依傍南屏山麓，寺内钟声远播杭州城，成"西湖十景"之一，名为"南屏晚钟"。

Gold Fish of Hangzhou

While China is the home of gold fish, Hangzhou is their birthplace. As early as over 900 years ago, gold fish were discovered at the Pagoda of Six Realms and Nanping Hill by the Song dynasty poets Su Shunqin and Su Dongpo, one after the other. Both had written poems about gold fish.

杭州金鱼

中国是金鱼的故乡，杭州则是金鱼的发源地。早在900多年前，北宋诗人苏舜钦和苏东坡都先后在六和塔与南屏山发现金鱼并作诗记之。

Princes Bay Park

The park used to be the graveyard of Zhuangwen and Jingxian, two princes of the Song dynasty. It was converted into a park with unadorned scenery in the late 1980s. The large-scale display of tulips held here every spring is visited by crowds of people.

太子湾公园

旧为宋庄文、景献两太子葬地，80年代后期辟为公园。景观原始质朴，每年春都有大型郁金香花展，游人如潮。

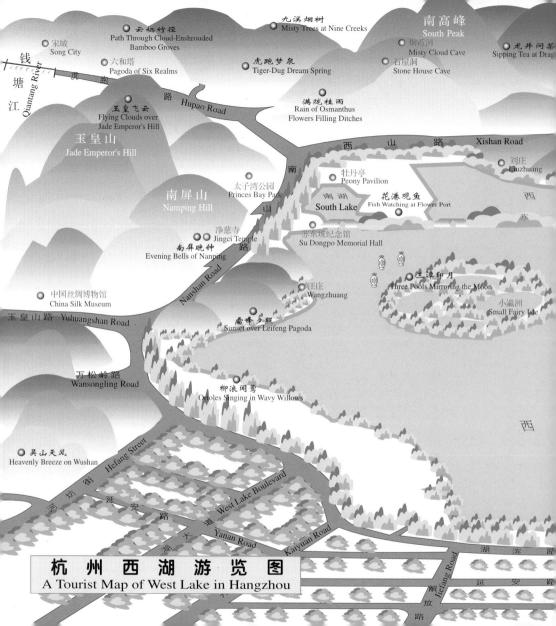

钱塘江
Qiantang River

宋城
Song City

云栖竹径
Path Through Cloud-Enshrouded
Bamboo Groves

九溪烟树
Misty Trees at Nine Creeks

南高峰
South Peak

烟霞洞
Misty Cloud Cave

龙井问茶
Sipping Tea at Drag

六和塔
Pagoda of Six Realms

虎跑梦泉
Tiger-Dug Dream Spring

石屋洞
Stone House Cave

虎跑路 Hupao Road

玉皇飞云
Flying Clouds over
Jade Emperor's Hill

满陇桂雨
Rain of Osmanthus
Flowers Filling Ditches

玉皇山
Jade Emperor's Hill

西山路 Xishan Road

牡丹亭
Peony Pavilion

刘庄
Liuzhuang

太子湾公园
Princes Bay Park

南屏山
Namping Hill

南湖
South Lake

花港观鱼
Fish Watching at Flower Port

南山路

西

苏堤

净慈寺
Jingci Temple

苏东坡纪念馆
Su Dongpo Memorial Hall

南屏晚钟
Evening Bells of Nanping

三潭印月
Three Pools Mirroring the Moon

汪庄
Wangzhuang

小瀛洲
Small Fairy Isle

中国丝绸博物馆
China Silk Museum

玉皇山路 Yuhuangshan Road

雷峰夕照
Sunset over Leifeng Pagoda

西

万松岭路
Wansongling Road

柳浪闻莺
Orioles Singing in Wavy Willows

吴山天风
Heavenly Breeze on Wushan

河坊街 Hefang Street

延安路

West Lake Boulevard

湖滨

延安

Yanan Road

开元路 Kaiyuan Road

解放路 Jiefang Road

杭州西湖游览图
A Tourist Map of West Lake in Hangzhou

中天竺
Middle Tianzhu

天竺路 Tianzhu Road

三天竺
Lower Tianzhu

茶叶博物馆
Tea Museum

灵隐路 Lingyin Road

北高峰
North Peak

灵隐寺
Lingyin Temple

飞来峰石窟
Flying-in Peak Grottoes

双峰插云
Twin Peaks Piercing the Clouds

杭州植物园
Hangzhou Botanical Garden

玉泉路 Yuquan Road

ongjing Road

郭庄
Guozhuang

曲院风荷
Lotus in the Breeze
in Curved Courtyard

岳湖
Yue Lake

栖霞洞
Cloud-Hovering Cave

岳王庙
Yue Fei's Temple

West Inner Lake

黄龙吐翠
Yellow Dragon
Spitting Green

堤
Su's Causeway

史春晓
Spring Morning on Su's Causeway

北

跨虹桥
Rainbow Rising Bridge

山

初阳台
Chuyang Terrace

阮公墩
Ruan's Mound

阮墩环碧
Ruan's Mound Surrounded
by Green

西泠印社
Xiling Seal Engraving Society

孤山
Solitary Hill

西泠桥
Xiling Bridge

路

保俶塔
Baoshu Pagoda

楼外楼餐馆
Louwailou Restaurant

文澜阁
Hall of Flourishing Literature

湖心亭
Lake Centre Pavilion

浙江博物馆
Zhejiang Museum

放鹤亭
Crane-Keeping Pavilion

北里湖
North Inner Lake

Beishan Road

宝石流霞
Fleeting Rosy Clouds over
Holy Stone Hill

平湖秋月
Autumn Moon over Calm Lake

白

湖

堤

断桥残雪
Traces of Snow on Broken Bridge

Bai's Causeway

保俶路 Baoshu Road

湖滨公园 Lakeside Park

Hubin Road

Pinghai Road

Yanan Road

Qingchun Road

环城西路 Western Ring Road

庆春路

平海路

图书在版编目（CIP）数据

西子湖畔: 英汉对照／张克庆摄影; 陈明钊撰文. – 北京: 外文出版社，2001
ISBN 7-119-02826-X

Ⅰ. 西… Ⅱ. ①张…②陈… Ⅲ. 名胜古迹 – 杭州市 – 摄影集 Ⅳ. K928.705.51–64
中国版本图书馆 CIP 数据核字(2001)第 00294 号

Photos by: Zhang Keqing

Text by: Chen Mingzhao

Translated by: Tang Bowen

Designed by: Yuan Qing

Edited by: Lan Peijing

摄影：张克庆

撰文：陈明钊

翻译：汤博文

设计：元　青

责任编辑：兰佩瑾

西子湖畔

张克庆　摄影

First Edition 2001

On the Shore of West Lake

ISBN 7-119-02826-X

© Foreign Languages Press
Published by Foreign Languages Press
24 Baiwanzhuang Road, Beijing 100037, China
Home Page: http://www.flp.com.cn
E-mail Addresses: info@flp.com.cn
　　　　　　　　sales@flp.com.cn
Printed in the People's Republic of China

© 外文出版社
外文出版社出版
（中国北京百万庄大街24号）
邮政编码：100037
外文出版社网页：http://www.flp.com.cn
外文出版社电子件邮件地址：info@flp.com.cn
　　　　　　　　　　　　sales@flp.com.cn
利丰雅高制作（深圳）有限公司印刷
北京骏马行图文中心制作
2001 年(24开)第一版
2001 年第一版第一次印刷
（英汉）
ISBN 7-119-02826-X/J · 1557（外）
004800（精）